COME & SEE

EXPLORING THE NAMES
OF JESUS FROM ISAIAH 9:6

COME
& SEE

BIBLE READINGS,
DISCUSSION
& CREATIVE
ACTIVITIES FOR
ADVENT

BETH MEVERDEN
& JENNA HALLOCK

10 Publishing
a division of 10 of those.com

British Library Cataloguing in Publication Data. A record for this book is available from the British Library

ISBN: 978-1-915705-30-3

Designed by Pete Barnsley (CreativeHoot.com)

Printed in the UK

10Publishing, a division of 10ofthose.com

Unit C, Tomlinson Road, Leyland, PR25 2DY, England

Email: info@10ofthose.com

Website: www.10ofthose.com

1 3 5 7 10 8 6 4 2

CONTENTS

WELCOME

MERRY CHRISTMAS!

For many of us, Christmas is the best time of the year. Warm memories and festive decorations make us feel peaceful and joyful. But for others, Christmas can be a sad or busy time of the year, seeming to lack peace and joy. As Christians, our external circumstances are only part of our experience. It is the hope we have in Jesus Christ that buoys our hearts and minds throughout the year and this Christmas season.

"Come and See" is our theme for this Family Advent Guide because as we teach our children and learn more ourselves, we want to invite others to know Jesus, too! As parents, our desire is for our children to come and see Jesus. This should lead us as a family to tell others about the Good News of Jesus Christ.

As you focus on Jesus through learning the names given to Him in Isaiah 9:6, our prayer is that everyone in the family will come and rest in God's Word this Christmas and see Jesus more clearly as they walk with Him daily.

Blessings to your family as you celebrate our Wonderful Counselor, Mighty God, Everlasting Father, Prince of Peace! Our God truly is Immanuel, God with us.

Jenna Hallock

Director of Community Engagement

Colorado Christian University

HOW TO USE THIS FAMILY ADVENT GUIDE

This Family Advent Guide contains four sessions to do together throughout Advent and an extra fifth session for after Christmas. The weekly "Family Time" slot is where you all come together to read the Bible, pray, learn and worship. Many families struggle to find a devotional time each day but a weekly Family Time can be more manageable. You should allow 20 minutes for Family Time but you're welcome to take longer if you'd like.

Deuteronomy 6:6–9 exhorts us to teach God's Word to our children at every opportunity. We hope that you will build upon the foundations laid during Family Time to dwell on the biblical truths you've learnt throughout the week. Each session ends with some more suggestions for how to do this at other times, specifically while you're on the go, at play time, dinner time and bed time.

COME AND SEE

Each session starts with Parent Time to help you to prepare spiritually and practically for Family Time. Read the devotional ahead of time to prepare your heart and mind and spend a few minutes praying for each of your children. Doing the practical preparations will help your Family Time to run smoothly, too.

Decide on a day each week that you'll do Family Time. Sundays would be the traditional time, but you can do it whenever works best. Choose somewhere comfortable to meet where there will be minimal distractions. Each session begins with an introduction. This will help prepare everyone for what you'll be looking at. You can make this really festive by lighting an Advent candle before you pray together.

There are two discussion slots in each Family Time. Discussion One (the main discussion) comes before the activity and Discussion Two (more application focused) is after the activity. The discussion time has been designed to be easily adapted to each family. You'll notice that questions are aimed at "Little Ones" (simple questions), "Bigger Ones" (more complex questions) and "teens and adults" (thought-provoking discussion starters for teenagers and grown-ups). If you have a mixture of ages and abilities in your family then feel free to pick and choose the questions that work best for you.

In between discussion sessions you'll be instructed to complete the activity. This is a fun way of reinforcing the teaching and helps to break up the discussion for any restless ones! All preparation instructions have been provided and can be found in the Parent Time section.

Family Time concludes with a time to memorize the key Scripture and to pray together. Some top tips to help with Scripture memorization can be found at the back of the book. A set "call and response" prayer is included in this section. You may not be as familiar with this prayer style but it is another useful tool to help reinforce the truths you're learning together.

It is our prayer that you will use the contents of this devotional in the way that works best for your family and that it will prove a useful resource for you as you invite your family to come and see Jesus this Advent.

WONDERFUL COUNSELOR

 **TEACHING GOAL**

To understand that Jesus is our Wonderful Counselor and we can trust Him completely to guide us in our lives because He is Wisdom itself.

PARENT TIME

♥ PREPARE YOUR HEART

Over the next few weeks we will be preparing our children to celebrate Christ's coming and His return throughout the Advent Season.

Our key verse this Advent will be Isaiah 9:6, focusing on a different key name each week. This week we will be looking at Jesus as our Wonderful Counselor.

> For to us a child is born,
>> to us a son is given,
>> and the government will be on his shoulders.
> And he will be called
>> **Wonderful Counselor**, Mighty God,
>> Everlasting Father, Prince of Peace.

Isaiah, the author of this prophecy, was writing around 700 years before the birth of Jesus. It was a time of fear and uncertainty for God's people as Judah was under threat from the superpower of the time, Assyria. Many of God's people had turned away from the Lord, refusing to repent and follow His commands. Ahaz, king of Judah, put his trust in an allegiance with Assyria rather than in God.

Isaiah speaks into this dark and fearful backdrop and, with his promise of a coming Wonderful Counselor, points Judah to their future King who would always lead them wisely because He would be God Himself. Where Ahaz had failed to walk with the Lord and be wise, the promised King would be their source of ultimate wisdom and counsel in any circumstance.

Isaiah's words give hope to those of us who need wisdom! Do you feel like you could use some wisdom? We also face threats, fear, and the temptation to trust in our own strength. Maybe the month ahead has you anxious about finances, relationships, managing the family schedule, meeting year-end work goals, or any number of struggles completely unrelated to this time of year.

No matter your worries or joys at this moment, God has promised us the wisdom He gives as our Wonderful Counselor. James tells us, "If any of you lacks wisdom, you should ask God, who gives generously to all without finding fault, and it will be given to you" (James 1:5).

We need to be reminded of this daily; moment by moment, even. God promises He will give us wisdom – generous portions of wisdom – and will not find fault in our asking. Let that truth sit in your heart and mind for just a moment. Take a long breath and savor that good promise from your Wonderful Counselor.

What specific thing(s) do you need your Wonderful Counselor to speak wisdom into right now? Have you asked Him for help? If not, stop right now and ask! If you have, look to see how He provides. Take a moment and write down your request, then write out James 1:5 below or on some paper in a place where you will see it daily.

PRAY

God of all Wisdom, I need Your insight and guidance in training and leading my children through this study and every day. Please use this devoted time to grant my children "the wisdom and understanding that the Spirit gives" (Colossians 1:9). I am so grateful for You.

In Jesus' Name, Amen.

PREPARE PRACTICALLY

The activity for Session One is a progressive treasure hunt. You will hide clues around the house that will guide your children to the hidden treasure – ingredients needed to make hot chocolate.

INSTRUCTIONS

To prepare the progressive treasure hunt you will first need to write each clue out on a piece of paper. Keep the first clue to hand out when the activity commences.

Next, hide each item (in bold below) in the suggested location, along with the clue for the next location. You could decide to put the ingredients into containers so your children don't guess what they are making right away. A blindfold may help to make it more difficult for older children.

CLUE 1: I AM NICE AND COZY IN YOUR FAVORITE PLACE TO SNUGGLE UP.

Place the **mugs** in a cozy spot e.g. a couch, bed, or chair.

CLUE 2: I AM CAMOUFLAGED AS SOIL, THE FOUNDATION OF GROWING GOOD THINGS.

Place the packaged **hot chocolate mix** on top of a planter or anywhere with dirt.

CLUE 3: I AM STEAMING AND HOT AND IN A TEAPOT.

Fill a **teapot or kettle** with water ready to be boiled when found.

CLUE 4: I AM IN THE FRONT HALL DISGUISED AS A SNOWBALL/ I AM BY THE FRONT DOOR LIKE SNOW ON THE FLOOR.

Hide the **marshmallows** in the front hall.

FAMILY TIME

📄 INTRODUCTION

Our theme for Advent this year is "Come and See." We want to learn more about Jesus so we can see Him more clearly and invite those who don't know Him to come and see Him as He really is!

Who knows what "Advent" means?

Advent is the hope and anticipation of Christ's return as we celebrate His birth.

It's like when we look forward to (or anticipate) celebrating someone's birthday or a special event. Every year we remember the birth of Jesus Christ at Christmas and celebrate that God sent His Son to Earth for us.

What do we do to prepare for someone's birthday in our family?

One thing we can do to celebrate someone's birthday is to light candles. We are going to do that same thing each week by lighting one special Advent candle.

This week as we light the candle we remember that God is our Wonderful Counselor and He can be trusted.

PRAY

Lord Jesus, thank You that You came and You are returning. We need Your wisdom and counsel in our lives in this and every season. We celebrate You! In Your Name, Amen.

DISCUSSION ONE

This verse from the Bible tells us about what Jesus is like.

The verse comes from the book of Isaiah. Isaiah was a prophet who talked about Jesus coming to Earth even though he lived a long time before Jesus was born. Isaiah tells us about some special names Jesus would be given …

READ ISAIAH 9:6

For to us a child is born,
to us a son is given,
and the government will be on his shoulders.
And he will be called
Wonderful Counselor, Mighty God,
Everlasting Father, Prince of Peace.

QUESTIONS FOR LITTLE ONES

- Can you think of something wonderful? Tell us about it.
- Who do you ask when you need help?
- Can you think of anyone Jesus helped in the Bible?
- Did you know that Jesus can help us today?

QUESTIONS FOR BIGGER ONES

- Did you hear the first name Isaiah uses to describe Jesus?

  Wonderful Counselor.

- What do you think "wonderful" means?

  We use wonderful to mean something really great, lovely or awesome. Here the word is stronger – Jesus will be better than anything we can imagine!

- What does a counselor do?

  A counselor is someone who helps us. They give advice or guidance.

- Can you give an example of some wise advice that you were given? How did you know to trust that advice?

  Wise people give us good advice and they can be trusted.

- If you were making a speech to introduce Jesus today how would you describe Him?

 ## QUESTIONS FOR TEENS AND ADULTS

- Often, we trust what someone says because they have been proved right in the past. Isaiah's prophecy, "A child will be born to us," came true when Jesus was born. Can you think of examples of how Isaiah was right about Jesus being a Wonderful Counselor too?

- In the New Testament, the Holy Spirit is described as a helper or counselor (see John 14:26). What difference does it make to know that the Spirit of the Wonderful Counselor lives in you?

ACTIVITY

We are going to go on a treasure hunt around the house following some guiding "counsel" (clues). Each clue will lead us to a part of the treasure and the next clue. When we get to the end, we will put all the parts we find together for a good and yummy treasure. Come and see the good treasure I have for you!

Hand your child the first clue to help them get to the first part of the treasure hunt. For younger children you can read each clue for them, and give hints if they need help figuring it out. You can also play hot and cold if your child needs extra help.

DISCUSSION TWO

 ## QUESTIONS FOR LITTLE ONES

- What was the good treasure you found?

- Jesus is the best treasure. How is Jesus better than the hot chocolate treasure?

- How can you ask Jesus to help you and when can you ask Him?

 ## QUESTIONS FOR BIGGER ONES

- Were the treasure hunt clues easy and helpful, or confusing and tricky? *Our (imperfect) treasure hunt clues in this game are a reminder that Jesus is our Wonderful Counselor who will lead us perfectly throughout our lives – He gives us much better guidance than the clues and much better treasure too.*

- What is the good treasure to which Jesus leads us?

  The best treasure is Jesus Himself. If we trust Him we can know and enjoy His goodness and wisdom every day for eternity!

- How does Jesus being a Wonderful Counselor make Him better than other leaders we might follow?

  Jesus will never let us down because of His great love for us. He doesn't just give wise advice – He is wisdom itself (1 Cor. 1:30). He will always lead us the right way, so we can trust Him 100%.

- How can we be wise like Jesus?

  We can learn His wisdom by reading the Bible, praying, and talking to wise people who trust Him. We can ask God for His wisdom too. James 1:5 says, "If any of you lacks wisdom, you should ask God, who gives generously to all without finding fault, and it will be given to you."

- Is there anything you need to ask Jesus to help you with now?

 ## QUESTIONS FOR TEENS AND ADULTS

- Do you find it easy to go to Jesus when you face difficulties?
- How might you cultivate dependence on Jesus' wisdom in your life?

MEMORIZE

Spend some moments introducing the Advent memory verse and begin memorizing in any way you choose.

For to us a child is born,
    to us a son is given,
    and the government will be on his shoulders.
And he will be called
    Wonderful Counselor, Mighty God,
    Everlasting Father, Prince of Peace.

(Isaiah 9:6)

PRAY

Dear God, thank You that Jesus is our Wonderful Counselor who is always there to listen to us and help us make wise choices. Thank You that Jesus is trustworthy. Help us to look to Him when we need guidance, advice, and counsel. We love You and want others to come and see You this Christmas season.

In Your Name, Amen.

Parent: Jesus, You are our Wonderful Counselor.
Child: Please guide us, Jesus.

Parent: Jesus, You are wise and loving.
Child: Please guide us, Jesus.

Parent: Jesus, You are trustworthy and faithful.
Child: Please guide us, Jesus.

Parent: Jesus, You are our Wonderful Counselor.
Child: Please guide us, Jesus.

IDEAS FOR THE WEEK AHEAD

 ## PLAY TIME

Play the treasure hunt game again but switch roles and help your child write and hide the clues for the rest of the family to find.

 ## GO TIME

Make hot chocolate mix (or a little basket with hot chocolate packets and marshmallows) to take to a neighbor with an invitation to one of your church's Christmas services or events.

 ## MEAL TIME

Practice saying Isaiah 9:6 together while you eat a family meal. You might like to share how remembering that Jesus is our Wonderful Counselor is making a difference in your week.

BED TIME

Consider making or purchasing "prayer journals" for each family member. Decorate the cover with the words "Jesus is my Wonderful Counselor." Encourage family members to talk to God in prayer using their journal each day during Advent.

MIGHTY GOD

 ## TEACHING GOAL

To understand that Jesus is our strong and Mighty God. He has the power to rescue us from sin and to help us in our weakness.

PARENT TIME

♥ PREPARE YOUR HEART

For to us a child is born,
to us a son is given,
and the government will be on his shoulders.
And he will be called
*Wonderful Counselor, **Mighty God**,*
Everlasting Father, Prince of Peace.

Isaiah prophesied that the coming Savior would be "Mighty God" to a people under threat of siege and captivity. Israel had forgotten the Lord and were terrified, with only weak king Ahaz to lead them; they needed to hear this promise of a future strong and mighty leader.

The promised Messiah would be "Mighty God", a divine king from the Davidic line (Jeremiah 23:5) who wouldn't be limited by His human strength.

Jesus exhibited His might in His first coming through His power over sickness, the world He created, and even the power over death He showed us at the resurrection. His might will be seen even more fully in His second coming. When He comes again, we will see all His incomparable strength, never-ending power and might as He judges the world and brings us into His prepared kingdom. That's a great reason to celebrate the Advent (coming) of Christ our King.

Even as adults, we often feel weak. It's become a running joke with people of a certain age that you no longer have to do any strenuous activity to hurt yourself; all you have to do is sleep the wrong way!

How incredible that Jesus, Mighty God, is able to identify with us in our weaknesses because He experienced human frailty first-hand. Our Mighty God became a baby that first Christmas, the weakest of the weak, in order to powerfully rescue us. In the flesh, He felt our weakness and overcame it.

As we get older, we also recognize how much we need God and His strength in every area of our lives. We need Him to help us and lead us every day in every way. As the song "Jesus loves me" says, "[we] are weak but He is strong."

Our Mighty God offers us His strength right now. Proverbs 18:10 reminds us: "The name of the Lord is a fortified tower; the righteous run to it and are safe." What would it look like to run to the safety of our Mighty God today? Are you broken by your sin? Run to Him! Are you suffering from physical pain? Run to Him! Do you feel your mind is betraying you? Run to Him!

We want our children to see that we are dependent on our Mighty God and not on ourselves. You can take shelter in Him against the war raging in and around you. He will not forsake those who belong to Him.

Have you experienced the might and power of God in your life? Take a moment to praise Him for how He has already provided for you. If you are feeling powerless right now, ask Him to give you His power to keep going, that He would receive the glory!

PRAY

Mighty God, You are God over every aspect of our lives. When we are weak, You are strong. Please give us Your strength and wisdom to train our children in Your ways and teach them of Your power, might and love through this Family Time Activity and throughout the week.

In Jesus' Name, Amen.

PREPARE PRACTICALLY

This session's activity will be to build a fort with a roof so that you can gaze up at some Christmas light "stars." To prepare gather together everything you need to build a fort and put the items in the space you will use.

MATERIALS

- Chairs (or other items to provide structural support)
- Blankets
- Dark colored sheet (to use for the roof)
- String of Christmas lights
- Pillows
- Flashlight (torch)
- Clothes pins (pegs) or other item to secure sheets/blankets
- Snacks to eat in your fort (optional)

FAMILY TIME

 REVIEW

What name of Jesus did we talk about in the last session? *Wonderful Counselor.*

 INTRODUCTION

Today we light our candle to remind us that Jesus is our Mighty God.

Turn off the other lights in the room and look at the candle for a moment. Just like this tiny candle lights up the room, the power of Jesus is strong and powerful to bring light into a dark world.

PRAY

Lord Jesus, thank You that You are so much stronger than we are and that You love us. Please show us what it means that You are Mighty God through this study.

In Your Name, Amen.

DISCUSSION ONE

Start by inviting a family member to read Isaiah 9:6. Then, try to say the verse together without looking at the words.

> *For to us a child is born,*
> *to us a son is given,*

and the government will be on his shoulders.
And he will be called
Wonderful Counselor, Mighty God,
Everlasting Father, Prince of Peace.

⬛ QUESTIONS FOR LITTLE ONES

- Mighty means really strong. What is the strongest thing you can think of? *Whatever their answer, say all together, "Jesus is stronger!"*

- Sometimes little things contain something surprising. Can you think of any examples? *Nesting Dolls, Piñata, a plant seed, a smart phone/tablet.*

- Jesus looked just like an ordinary baby but He was also Mighty God. *Say all together, "Wow! That's amazing!"*

⬛⬛ QUESTIONS FOR BIGGER ONES

- What is the second name Isaiah uses to describe Jesus in this verse?

  Mighty God.

- What do you think "mighty" means?

  Having great and impressive power or strength.

- What do you think of when you hear the word "mighty?"

  There are lots of powerful things in our world, but nothing is more powerful than Jesus.

- Imagine being a Jewish person under Roman occupation. What would you expect a Mighty Messiah to do?

  Defeat the Romans.

- How did Jesus show that He was Mighty God?

  Through His power over nature, sickness, and death. Ultimately His death and resurrection has defeated our greatest enemy – much more powerful than defeating the Romans!

 ## QUESTIONS FOR TEENS AND ADULTS

- Spend a few moments pondering that Jesus was Mighty God at His birth, in His earthly life, death and resurrection. Do you think of Him this way at each of those points? Is it easy for you to believe that He is mighty?

- How much do you value strength in your own life? Do you value physical, mental, or spiritual strength more and why? How does Jesus show strength in weakness? Consider 2 Corinthians 12:10 – is this how you approach weakness?

ACTIVITY

We are going to build a fort then we will look up at the "stars" to remind us that the Mighty God who made the world became a baby to rescue us.

Make a fort big enough for everyone to fit inside using chairs, pillows, blankets, and whatever else works for fort building in your home. Place a dark sheet over the top of the fort then place a string of Christmas lights (spread out like stars in the sky) on top of the blanket. Place a blanket on the ground and have everyone go into the fort and turn off the other lights in the house. Use a flashlight (torch) to read the rest of the lesson. Pause to enjoy a snack after constructing your fort if you like.

Spend a few moments looking up at the Christmas light "stars." Remind your children that the Mighty God who made the stars became a baby at Christmastime!

DISCUSSION TWO

 QUESTIONS FOR LITTLE ONES

- Was it tricky to make the fort?

- How does it feel when someone you love helps you?

  Little ones will need help building the fort – an opportunity to point to the Mighty God who is powerful to help us.

- Did you like being in the fort? How did it make you feel?

  We can remember feeling safe and happy in the fort and looking up at the stars when we feel afraid. The Mighty God who made the stars loves and cares for us.

- What are some things God can help us with? How do we know He can help us?

  God is Mighty. He is able to help us even more than Mommy/ Daddy/trusted friend because He is strong!

QUESTIONS FOR BIGGER ONES

- Did you need to be strong to build the fort?

- How strong are we compared to Jesus?

- What is your biggest weakness or problem? How can Jesus help?

  Jesus is Mighty God and has dealt with our biggest problem of sin through His death and resurrection. He knows all our weaknesses and nothing we struggle with is too big for Him to deal with.

- Is there anything you need to ask Jesus to help you with right now?

 ## QUESTIONS FOR TEENS AND ADULTS

- In what areas of your life are you tempted to rely on your own strength?

- How will knowing Jesus is Mighty God help in your battle against sin?

MEMORIZE

For to us a child is born,
*   to us a son is given,*
*   and the government will be on his shoulders.*
And he will be called
*   Wonderful Counselor, Mighty God,*
*   Everlasting Father, Prince of Peace.*

(Isaiah 9:6)

PRAY

Dear God, thank You that Jesus is our Mighty God and stronger than anything else in our lives, including our sin. Bring to mind the people who need to know Your strength and love this week. We love You. We celebrate You.

In Your Name, Amen.

Parent: Jesus, You are Mighty God.

Child: Please give us Your strength, Jesus.

Parent: Jesus, You are Strong.

Child: Please give us Your strength, Jesus.

Parent: Jesus, You are the all-powerful Creator.

Child: Please give us Your strength, Jesus.

Parent: Christ Jesus, I can run to You and You will give me strength.

Child: Please give us Your strength, Jesus.

Parent: Jesus, when I am afraid, You give me strength.

Child: Please give us Your strength, Jesus.

Parent: Jesus, You are Mighty God.

Child: Please give us Your strength, Jesus.

IDEAS FOR THE WEEK AHEAD

PLAY TIME

Teach your children the song "My God is so Big" with its hand motions. Simply search the title and you'll find many versions of the song online. This fabulous song talks about God being big and mighty and reminds us to trust in Him.

GO TIME

Drive past or take a walk to the tallest/oldest/strongest buildings in your town. Talk about how God is mightier than anything men can build or imagine. You could invite some friends on the adventure and tell each other what it means that Jesus is Mighty.

MEAL TIME

For dessert, provide marshmallows and toothpicks and have a challenge to see who can build the strongest marshmallow tower. Set a timer, if preferred. Once a winner is declared, heat chocolate for dipping the marshmallows.

BED TIME

Praise God for being mighty. Ask Him to protect us even as we sleep. For little ones, give them imagery that will fill their dreamy minds with the protection of their Mighty God!

EVERLASTING FATHER

 ## TEACHING GOAL

To understand that Jesus is the promised King who will love His people like a father loves his children.

PARENT TIME

♥ PREPARE YOUR HEART

For to us a child is born,
to us a son is given,
and the government will be on his shoulders.
And he will be called
Wonderful Counselor, Mighty God,
***Everlasting Father**, Prince of Peace.*

Isaiah chapter 9 begins by referring to God's people as "in distress," and "walking in darkness." They had constantly rejected God, and He had removed His hand of protection and allowed His people to experience the consequences of their disobedience. However, it was to this people that Isaiah also said the hopeful words, "For to us a child is born…"

What great love the Lord has for His people! He wouldn't abandon them to punishment but would send them the rescuing King they longed for. This King would be called "Everlasting Father." At first glance it seems like an odd name for a child, but it points to the divinity and perfect nature of the future King. It alludes to the Messiah's role as leader of a nation who would rule, protect and provide (Isaiah 22:21).

Jesus is this Everlasting Father, Ruler, Protector, and Provider, and He rules a kingdom that will never end (Isaiah 9:7). We have never seen a ruler like this. No government authority rules forever. No human father has rule over us forever, but Jesus' rule is infinite.

Some of us may struggle with the idea of Jesus being described as Father. We each have an imperfect earthly father – some godly and caring, others who let us down in myriad ways. Christmas events with family can often highlight the good and the bad of these relationships. When our human experience only affords us a broken picture of fatherhood, it can cloud how we see this quality of Jesus.

It is good news, though, that Jesus is described as Everlasting Father. He is beyond comparison to any earthly father. He will always lead perfectly, and His fatherhood will be eternal. Colossians 1:17 tells us, "He is before all things, and in him all things hold together." He created. He sustains. He is unchanging.

The Everlasting Father who comes to us as the God-Man, Jesus Christ, is all-powerful, all-knowing, and full of grace and truth. He is King over all and has created a people for Himself by conquering sin and death.

Let's come and see Jesus for who He is. Luke 1:32–33 tells us, "He will be great and will be called the Son of the Most High. The Lord God will give him the throne of his father David, and He will reign over Jacob's descendants forever; his kingdom will never end." Jesus is the Everlasting Father we all need.

As you remember the promises of God through the birth of Jesus as "Everlasting Father", thank Him for His unchanging, eternal strength and care. Pray, too, that you can help your children to see how Jesus cares, leads, provides, and protects us as a father as you do your lesson this week.

PRAY

Lord Jesus, please lead us as we train our children to know you as Everlasting Father, Ruler, King, and Protector in this lesson. Take away any hurdles we have about what a father is and help us to see You clearly.

In Jesus' Name, Amen.

PREPARE PRACTICALLY

This week's activity is a sensory game where the children will have to guess which items have an evergreen smell. In advance, choose five items with a strong or easily identifiable smell and two items that have an evergreen scent.

Place each item in a separate paper bag.

During the activity the children will smell each bag to try and identify the items!

FAMILY TIME

REVIEW

Which names of Jesus have we already talked about as we've been celebrating Advent? *Wonderful Counselor and Mighty God.*

What have you learned this Christmas season about Jesus as our Wonderful Counselor and Mighty God?

Have you had the chance to invite anyone to come and see Jesus?

INTRODUCTION

We light our candle today to remember that Jesus is our Everlasting Father. This means that Jesus will always love us like a good father. Jesus will always be the light of the world that will never go out!

PRAY

Lord Jesus, thank You that You have always been and will always be God. Thank You that You are the light that never goes out in our lives! Please help us understand who You are as Everlasting Father as we learn about You today. Please give us guidance about how we can invite others to come and see You as Everlasting Father.

In Your Name, Amen.

DISCUSSION ONE

Practice your memory verse together.

> For to us a child is born,
>> to us a son is given,
>> and the government will be on his shoulders.
> And he will be called
>> Wonderful Counselor, Mighty God,
>> Everlasting Father, Prince of Peace. (Isaiah 9:6)

QUESTIONS FOR LITTLE ONES

- How does a good dad look after his children?

- *Jesus looks after His people like the best dad looks after his children.*

- How does it make you feel to know Jesus looks after you?

- Can you think of something that changes a lot? What is something in your life that never changes?

- *Jesus will always be a good leader who loves us like a dad. That will never change!*

QUESTIONS FOR BIGGER ONES

- What is the third name of Jesus in this verse? *Everlasting Father.*

- What clue does Isaiah give that the future king will be more than just a human king? *The Messiah will be an everlasting king. All the human Old Testament kings died but Jesus is God so will be a king forever.*

- 'Father' is a strange name to give a baby! What do you think this name tells us about Jesus? *'Father' reminds us of someone who loves and cares. In this passage it particularly means Jesus will be the perfect king who protects and provides for His people.*

- Can you think of a ruler or leader today or from history? What difference would it make/have made if they ruled their people like a good father?

 ## QUESTIONS FOR TEENS AND ADULTS

- Reflect on what you know about the Old Testament kings. Why would this prophecy about Jesus being the Everlasting Father have been good news for Isaiah's listeners?

- Read Luke 1:32–33. The everlasting King Jesus will rule forever like a father. What does that mean to you today?

ACTIVITY

Our sense of smell is a gift from God. Different scents can remind us of people, events, and even seasons!

What are some smells that remind you of springtime, summertime, fall (autumn), and winter/Christmas?

Play the sensory game! Ask everyone to close their eyes and then place each bag in turn under each person's nose. Have family members guess each smell. Can everyone identify the evergreen items?

DISCUSSION TWO

 QUESTIONS FOR LITTLE ONES

- Did you enjoy playing the smelling game? Why or why not?

- Do you like the evergreen smell?

- *The fun thing about evergreen trees (Christmas trees) is they don't change. Their leaves stay green all year round. When you next see a Christmas tree you can remember that Jesus doesn't change either – He will always love you!*

 QUESTIONS FOR BIGGER ONES

- We just smelled evergreen things. Do you know what makes evergreen trees special? *Evergreen trees stay green all year round.*

- *We can look at, smell, and touch Christmas trees this year and remind ourselves that Jesus doesn't change either. He is the perfect fatherly king forever!*

- Why is this good news?

- How do you think Jesus shows His fatherly love and care for us? *His death on the cross shows His sacrificial love. He still intercedes for us today, showing His ongoing care.*

 QUESTIONS FOR TEENS AND ADULTS

- Isaiah's readers would have been looking forward to a king who would perfectly protect and provide for them. How has Jesus fulfilled this prophecy and how will it ultimately be fulfilled at His second coming?

- Often we can struggle with the word 'father' in relation to God because of our own experiences of our earthly fathers. Has that clouded your view of the good news contained in the promise that Jesus loves like a father? Ask Jesus to help you see His fatherly protection and provision as something to celebrate this Christmas.

MEMORIZE

For to us a child is born,
  to us a son is given,
    and the government will be on his shoulders.
And he will be called
    Wonderful Counselor, Mighty God,
    Everlasting Father, Prince of Peace.

(Isaiah 9:6)

PRAY

Dear Jesus, thank You that You came to be the King who would love us like a father forever. When things around us change, remind us that You are in charge and that You will always love us.

In Your Name, Amen.

Parent:	Jesus, You are Everlasting Father.
Child:	Thank You for being with us, Jesus.
Parent:	Jesus, You rule as the perfect King.
Child:	Thank You for being with us, Jesus.
Parent:	Jesus, You do not change like shifting shadows.
Child:	Thank You for being with us, Jesus.
Parent:	Jesus, You are Immanuel, God with us.
Child:	Thank You for being with us, Jesus.
Parent:	Jesus, You have always been, will always be and are with us now.
Child:	Thank You for being with us, Jesus.
Parent:	Jesus, You are Everlasting Father.
Child:	Thank You for being with us, Jesus.

IDEAS FOR THE WEEK AHEAD

PLAY TIME

Decorate a cut out Christmas tree using green construction paper, glitter, markers, etc. or cut a tree out of green cellophane or tissue paper and hang it in a window as a reminder that Jesus is our Everlasting Father.

GO TIME

Walk around your neighborhood to view Christmas light displays. You could make and distribute cards that say, "We think your Christmas tree is the most (beautiful/creative/sparkly/festive) in the neighborhood. Thank you for spreading Christmas cheer! Merry Christmas!" Or simply have a chat about the lights and trees you see and reflect on Jesus being our Everlasting Father.

MEAL TIME

Serve vegetables to create a Christmas tree. Broccoli for branches, small tomatoes for lights, baby carrots for the trunk, cauliflower for "snow" on the branches and a few yellow bell pepper slices to make a star on top. Provide hummus or salad dressing for dipping.

BED TIME

Light an evergreen scented candle as you are getting everyone ready for bed. Ask your child what the smell reminds them of from your Family Time Activity.

PRINCE OF PEACE

 **TEACHING GOAL**

To understand that Jesus has given us peace with God through His death. He also helps us with our daily worries and concerns.

PARENT TIME

❤ PREPARE YOUR HEART

For to us a child is born,
   to us a son is given,
   and the government will be on his shoulders.
And he will be called
   Wonderful Counselor, Mighty God,
   *Everlasting Father, **Prince of Peace.***

In Isaiah chapter 8, Isaiah predicts Assyria's subjugation of Judah. King Ahaz thought he had bought his nation peace through an allegiance with Assyria, but his rejection of God and His ways would lead to oppression and captivity. Isaiah goes on to prophesy to a troubled people in chapter 9 of a coming Messiah who would be their "Prince of Peace."

When Jesus did arrive on the scene, tragically many people didn't recognize Him as Messiah. They had wrong expectations of peace, and they underestimated what they needed rescuing from. They wanted to be free from Roman rule and political tyranny and didn't understand that sin and death were their greater problem. Jesus' death on a cross was not what they expected from their King. The cross looked like a catastrophic defeat, but, in reality, it was an unrivaled victory, securing our eternal peace.

It is not uncommon to believe we can be the source of our own peace. We create times, spaces, rituals, and experiences that give us a sense of calm or relaxation but they only provide a respite from our current circumstances. They give us a momentary illusion of peace, but no matter where we are or what we are doing, our mind can carry us to places of anxiety and unrest. Like the people in Jesus' day, we underestimate the problem that needs fixing.

What we really need for true peace has been won for us already through Jesus' victory over sin and death. Colossians 1:19–20 speaks of our peace coming through Jesus' sacrifice on the cross, "For God was pleased to have all his fullness dwell in him, and through him to reconcile to himself all things, whether things on earth or things in heaven, by making peace through his blood, shed on the cross." This doesn't mean we won't encounter troubles and anxieties now, but Jesus Himself promises to give us His peace:

"Peace I leave with you; my peace I give you. I do not give to you as the world gives. Do not let your hearts be troubled and do not be afraid" (John 14:27).

"I have told you these things, so that in me you may have peace. In this world you will have trouble. But take heart! I have overcome the world" (John 16:33).

Where do we find true and lasting peace? Not in this world where we will have trouble! Our peace comes when we trust that Jesus has overcome sin and alienation from God. We cannot live in the light of this truth in our own strength. But, thankfully, God has provided a helper in the Holy Spirit who promises to cultivate love, joy, and peace in our lives.

What about the Christmas season brings you peace? What brings anxiety? Take a deep breath and hear the words of Jesus, "My peace I give you." Take a moment to reflect on this promise and how you desire to live it out in the days ahead.

PREPARE PRACTICALLY

If you'd like, you can get some warm blankets ready for Discussion Two.

The activity is to make a calming glitter jar to help remind our children that Jesus is our Prince of Peace.

MATERIALS

- Small jar
- Glitter
- Clear glue
- Warm water

If you are feeling extra creative, you can customize the calming glitter jars in lots of different ways. For example, you could add mini Christmas decorations, some larger sequins or sparkles, or even color the water with food coloring/dye.

FAMILY TIME

 REVIEW

What are the names of Jesus we have already talked about as we have been celebrating Advent? *Wonderful Counselor, Mighty God, and Everlasting Father.*

How have you been able to come and see Jesus in a new way by learning about His names?

INTRODUCTION

We light our candle today to remember that Jesus is our Prince of Peace. What is peace? *Ultimate peace is found in having a relationship with Jesus. This peace lasts no matter what is happening in our lives.*

PRAY

Lord God, thank You that Jesus is our peace no matter what is happening in our lives or in the world.

In His Name, Amen.

DISCUSSION ONE

Practice your memory verse together.

> *For to us a child is born,*
> *to us a son is given,*
> *and the government will be on his shoulders.*

And he will be called
  Wonderful Counselor, Mighty God,
  Everlasting Father, Prince of Peace. (Isaiah 9:6)

Ⓛ QUESTIONS FOR LITTLE ONES

- What makes you feel peaceful? What is the opposite of peace?

- Can you think of any heroes? (From books, movies, or TV shows.)

- Do they usually bring peace or trouble? *Talk about how some heroes bring fun and adventure but the best ones bring rescue and 'peace' to the person/community they are rescuing.*

- How does Jesus rescue us and give us peace with God? *By dying for us on the cross and coming alive again so we can be friends with God.*

QUESTIONS FOR BIGGER ONES

- What is the fourth name of Jesus in this verse? *Prince of Peace.*

- Why do you think God wanted Isaiah to tell everyone that Jesus would bring peace? *The Jewish people had been ruled by kings who hadn't brought them peace. The promise of a king who is peace itself would have been a great encouragement.*

- How would Jesus bring us ultimate peace? *He brought us peace with God through His death on the cross.*

- What are some ways that people create peace for themselves? Why is peace with God the most important kind of peace on offer to us? *Peace with God is the only peace that truly lasts and it's peace with our Creator – the most important person for us to be at peace with.*

- How can we be sure Jesus has given us peace with God? *He rose again, assuring us that He has taken care of our sin.*

 ## QUESTIONS FOR TEENS AND ADULTS

- An act of great atrocity and violence purchased our peace with God. Read Mark 15:15–39 substituting Jesus' name with "The Prince of Peace" and marvel again at what Jesus achieved for us on the cross.

- Do you despair over the lack of peace in our world? How might you turn that into longing for the Prince of Peace to return?

ACTIVITY

- Create your Christmas calming glitter jar.

- Add warm water, clear glue, and glitter to a jar, then mix well. Don't fill the jar right to the top, but leave a little space so it doesn't overflow. The more glue you add, the slower the glitter will fall.

- After the water has cooled a little, screw the lid on tightly. You can glue the lid on if you prefer.

- Give the jar a shake and watch the glitter fall!

DISCUSSION TWO

Shake your jar and think about a big blizzard. Think about the wind howling and blowing snow all around. Imagine the cold snow blowing on your face and giving you a chill. It makes you hunch your shoulders and want to curl up in a blanket, doesn't it? (Optional: Hand each person a warm blanket.)

This is how we can feel inside sometimes when we are worried. But when we pray and give those worries to Jesus, our Prince of Peace (place the jar on a flat surface), it can help us begin to calm down like the glitter storm in this jar is calming down.

Jesus gives us peace with God but He also cares about all our worries and difficulties and He promises to help us every day. When you are feeling upset, this glitter jar can remind you to pray to your Prince of Peace. You can shake the jar and pray, then set it down as a symbol of giving your worries to Jesus. While the glitter calms down, you can be reminded to trust Jesus to calm your heart and mind too.

READ JOHN 16:33

"I have told you these things, so that in me you may have peace. In this world you will have trouble. But take heart! I have overcome the world."

READ PHILIPPIANS 4:6-7

Do not be anxious about anything, but in every situation, by prayer and petition, with thanksgiving, present your requests to God. And the peace of God, which transcends all understanding, will guard your hearts and your minds in Christ Jesus.

QUESTIONS FOR LITTLE ONES

- Do you have any worries?
- Do you ever feel like the blizzard in the jar?

- What can you do when you're worried? *Encourage your child to talk to you about their worries and to talk to Jesus too!*

 ## QUESTIONS FOR BIGGER ONES

- What are some of the troubles we face? *Sickness, loss, transitions, limitations, disappointments, and all sorts of other things can cause us to feel troubled. The feelings these troubles bring are usually the opposite of peace and feel like a freezing cold blizzard that seems out of control all around us.*

- How can we have peace according to this verse? *Jesus says that in Him we can have peace because He has overcome the world. There's nothing that can happen to us that Jesus doesn't have power over.*

- What are some things that worry you? How do you usually cope with them? How can God give you peace?

- What is our ultimate hope in difficult times? *We can look forward to Jesus' second coming when pain, suffering, and worries will be no more!*

- Who could you pray for this week who particularly needs to know the peace Jesus offers?

 ## QUESTIONS FOR TEENS AND ADULTS

- How are your anxiety levels this Christmas? Do you model turning to Jesus in your fears and trials?

- What other things do you turn to for peace?

- How might you share God's peace with a non-Christian friend or family member this Christmas?

MEMORIZE

For to us a child is born,
  to us a son is given,
  and the government will be on his shoulders.
And he will be called
  Wonderful Counselor, Mighty God,
  Everlasting Father, Prince of Peace.

(Isaiah 9:6)

PRAY

Dear Jesus, thank You for being our Prince of Peace. Thank You that because of Your death on the cross we can have peace with God. Please help us with [name any worries or difficulties that have come up in the study]. Help us to know You are with us. Would You please help us see who needs Your peace and give us the courage to invite them to come and see You. Forgive us when we look to things besides You for our peace.

In Your Name, Amen.

Parent:	Jesus, You are Prince of Peace.
Child:	Thank You for Your peace, Jesus.
Parent:	Jesus, when I pray, You give me peace beyond my understanding.
Child:	Thank You for Your peace, Jesus.
Parent:	Jesus, You have overcome the world.
Child:	Thank You for Your peace, Jesus.
Parent:	Jesus, You do not give as the world gives.
Child:	Thank You for Your peace, Jesus.
Parent:	Jesus, Your peace is stronger than my feelings and circumstances.
Child:	Thank You for Your peace, Jesus.
Parent:	Jesus, You are Prince of Peace.
Child:	Thank You for Your peace, Jesus.

IDEAS FOR THE WEEK AHEAD

 ## PLAY TIME

Do a coloring activity where you play different kinds of music and have them color what they are hearing. Be sure to play more energetic music and gentler music then have the child describe his/her picture and how she or he was feeling as the different kinds of music were playing.

 ## GO TIME

Make a Christmas calming glitter jar and give it to someone you love. Include a note including this week's Scriptures.

 ## MEAL TIME

Just like shaking glitter jars, a blender is another visual reminder of how things can feel chaotic in our lives. Make frozen drinks with frozen fruit, juice, and yogurt or ice cream in a blender and talk about what your child learned about Jesus being the Prince of Peace as you enjoy the beverage together.

 ## BED TIME

Use your glitter jar to settle down for bed. Allow kids a certain number of shakes and when the glitter finally settles to the bottom the final time, say a prayer of peace over your family.

AFTER CHRISTMAS ...
SESSION FIVE:

COME AND SEE

 **TEACHING GOAL**

To understand God wants us to invite others to come and see Him in the New Year.

PARENT TIME

♥ PREPARE YOUR HEART

The next day Jesus decided to leave for Galilee. Finding Philip, he said to him, "Follow me."

Philip, like Andrew and Peter, was from the town of Bethsaida. Philip found Nathanael and told him, "We have found the one Moses wrote about in the Law, and about whom the prophets also wrote – Jesus of Nazareth, the son of Joseph."

"Nazareth! Can anything good come from there?" Nathanael asked.

"Come and see," said Philip (John 1:43–46).

How beautiful on the mountains are the feet of those who bring good news, who proclaim peace, who bring good tidings, who proclaim salvation, who say to Zion, "Your God reigns!" (Isaiah 52:7).

Decades passed before God's people went back to Israel after their prophesied exile and return. Centuries passed between Isaiah's prophecy of the Messiah and His arrival. Just as God's people longed for His first coming, we long for His second coming. Like the Israelites, we can get distracted and let our faithfulness, time with God, and telling others about Him wane.

It's easy to stop intentionally focusing on Jesus as Light of the World when the Christmas tree lights are boxed up and placed on the shelf. We often default to focusing on things we need to change in our own strength for the New Year.

Let's not give in to that temptation. Let's determine to come and see Jesus afresh this year as individuals and as a family. Let's ask God to show us how to continue the connections we made with our community during this study and consistently invite others to come and see Jesus through deeper relationship and time with our family.

PRAY

Lord God, please use this last study to fan the flame of our faith and keep our minds and hearts determined to invite others to come and see You for who You really are... Savior. We love and need You.

In Jesus' Name, Amen.

PREPARE PRACTICALLY

Assemble the blank cards and writing materials in advance.

FAMILY TIME

 REVIEW

Let's do a brief recap of what we've learned through this *Come and See* study together!

What did we learn about Jesus being Wonderful Counselor? What was your favorite part of that Family Time Activity?

What did we learn about Jesus being Mighty God? What are some things we talked about being mighty and strong?

What did we learn about Jesus being Everlasting Father? What are some things that can remind us of Jesus being everlasting?

What did we learn about Jesus being Prince of Peace? Is there anything we can do on our own to give us true peace?

Today we are going to take what we have learned and continue to make it practical.

📋 INTRODUCTION

It's easy to stop intentionally focusing on Jesus when the Christmas decorations are boxed up and placed on the shelf. We often default to thinking about things we need to change in our own strength for the New Year. Inviting others to come and see Jesus can feel like one of those things we need to find the strength to do on our own, but the good news is that Jesus will help us.

PRAY

Jesus, we need Your counsel to know who to share You with, and we need Your strength to overcome any fears we have about sharing You with others. God, we are so grateful You are everlasting, have always been and will always be with us. Thank You for granting us Your true peace and enabling us to share that peace and hope with others.

In Your Name, Amen.

DISCUSSION ONE

 ## READ JOHN 1:43-46

The next day Jesus decided to leave for Galilee. Finding Philip, he said to him, "Follow me."

Philip, like Andrew and Peter, was from the town of Bethsaida. Philip found Nathanael and told him, "We have found the one Moses wrote about in the Law, and about whom the prophets also wrote – Jesus of Nazareth, the son of Joseph."

"Nazareth! Can anything good come from there?" Nathanael asked.

"Come and see," said Philip.

QUESTIONS FOR LITTLE ONES

- Who did Philip find after he met Jesus? *Nathanael.*

- What is the last thing Philip says to Nathanael? *Come and see!*

- Did you get a special gift for Christmas? Did you want any friends or family to come and see it?

🎮 QUESTIONS FOR BIGGER ONES

- What did Philip tell Nathanael about Jesus? *"We have found the one Moses wrote about in the Law, and about whom the prophets also wrote – Jesus of Nazareth, the son of Joseph."*

- Choose the words that best describe how Nathanael reacted to Philip's information.

    1. Doubtful (skeptical)

    2. Disbelieving

    3. Immediate belief

- When Nathanael didn't believe Philip's words, what did Philip say to Nathanael? *Come and see!*

- Imagine seeing something special like a really tall Christmas tree, filled with lights and shimmering in the falling snow. Who would you want to share that with?

- We have an even greater thing to invite our friends to come and see, but that can sometimes feel tricky.

- Did Philip have to know a lot about Jesus to invite Nathanael to come and see? *Philip had only just met Jesus, he didn't know Jesus very well but he still shared with his friend. We don't need to worry about knowing all the answers in order to invite our friends to meet Jesus.*

QUESTIONS FOR TEENS AND ADULTS

- What stops you from inviting people to come and see Jesus? Ask for God's help in that area this year.

ACTIVITY

- Hand each family member a couple of cards.

- On each of your cards, write a name or draw a picture of someone you know who doesn't yet have a relationship with Jesus.

- When you are finished, turn all your cards face down and mix them all up like a deck of cards.

- Pick one card at a time and on the back, write one way you could tell each person about Jesus' love for them and invite them to come and see what Jesus has done and who He is.

- Some ideas:

  - Invite them to church, Sunday school or an outreach event.

  - Invite them to your house for a movie and snacks. Choose one of your favorite movies with a biblical message and talk about the movie's themes together.

  - Give them the gift of a Bible or Christian book.

  - Ask them if they'd like you to pray about anything.

  - Write them a card so they know you are praying for them. Share a specific Bible verse.

When you are finished writing the connection ideas on the back of each of the cards, place them somewhere you will see them regularly and be reminded to intentionally check in with each person throughout the rest of the year.

DISCUSSION TWO

 READ ISAIAH 52:7

> How beautiful on the mountains are the feet of those who bring good news, who proclaim peace, who bring good tidings, who proclaim salvation, who say to Zion, "Your God reigns!"

This is one of the Scripture passages that the song, "Go Tell it on the Mountain" is based on. It's a Christmas song, but it is also a reminder to go tell people about Jesus and invite them to come and see Him all throughout the year.

 FOR LITTLE ONES

- Listen to a recording of "Go Tell it on the Mountain" or sing it together if you prefer.

 FOR BIGGER ONES

- Before you listen to a recording of "Go Tell it on the Mountain", ask your children to be listening for the answer to this question:
  - Who were the obedient heroes who invited people to come and see Jesus in this true story?
- Then after the song ask:

- What have you learned in this study that will help you be more like the shepherds?

 ## GO TELL IT ON THE MOUNTAIN

Go, tell it on the mountain, over the hills and everywhere;
go, tell it on the mountain that Jesus Christ is born.

1. *While shepherds kept their watching*
   o'er silent flocks by night,
   behold, throughout the heavens
   there shone a holy light. [Refrain]

2. *The shepherds feared and trembled*
   when lo! above the earth
   rang out the angel chorus
   that hailed our Savior's birth. [Refrain]

3. *Down in a lowly manger*
   the humble Christ was born,
   and God sent us salvation
   that blessed Christmas morn.

 ## QUESTIONS FOR LITTLE ONES

- Who teaches you about Jesus?
- Can you remember something you have learned about Jesus this Advent?
- Who needs to know about Jesus?

 ## QUESTIONS FOR BIGGER ONES

- What reactions have you received when sharing the Good News about Jesus?

- How is Isaiah 52:7 an encouragement to keep sharing Jesus even when you don't get a positive reaction?
- Ask God to give you opportunities to share about Jesus this year.

 ## QUESTIONS FOR TEENS AND ADULTS

- Have John 1:43–46 and Isaiah 52:7 encouraged you in your evangelism? How can you take that encouragement forward into the new year?

MEMORIZE

Here's a new family memory verse to take you into the new year.

How beautiful on the mountains are the feet of those who bring good news, who proclaim peace, who bring good tidings, who proclaim salvation, who say to Zion, "Your God reigns!"

(Isaiah 52:7)

PRAY

Dear Jesus, thank You for this great reminder to be like Philip and to invite others to come and see who You are and what You are doing. Please give us courage to obey You when You give us opportunities to show and tell others about You.

In Your Name, Amen.

IDEAS FOR THE WEEK AHEAD

PLAY TIME

Give each other a pedicure or a foot massage as a reminder of the beauty of feet who go and tell others about Jesus. Or make some beautiful feet. Draw around your children's feet or shoes on some colored card and decorate your paper feet with beautiful gems/stickers/glitter.

GO TIME

When your church is starting a new program such as a Bible study or special event, grab a stack of invitations (or use a digital link) and share with at least one person who you have been praying for this month.

MEAL TIME

God calls some people to be missionaries to people and places around the world. If your family or your church supports a missionary, take time each day this week to pray for them before breakfast or dinner. If you are unsure where to start, we suggest Weave Family (weavefamily.org) or Open Doors (opendoors.org).

BED TIME

Hang one of the cards from earlier by a bed or even on the bathroom mirror until there has been an intentional connection with that person and then hang up the card of the next person.

WHAT NEXT?

As you conclude your time together going through this study, start thinking about the next study you can do as a family. There are many other wonderful resources available to help you to continue studying the Bible as a family; check out 10ofThose.com or FamTime.com for more ideas.

If your family enjoyed the focused time during the season of Advent, preparing to celebrate Easter through the season of Lent may be an organic next step.

Jesus is the ultimate source of everything we need in every area of our lives and our children need us to show them how to continue to follow Him. No matter what you choose to do, use the momentum of these special times together to continue to intentionally spiritually train your children and teens!

WHAT NEXT?

AUTHOR BIOS

Beth Meverden has been working in student and children's ministry for 25 years. She is delighted to be one of the regular blog writers for FamTime.com. She is a contributing activities writer for The Life of Christ curriculum, Seeing the Savior, An Advent Journey, and Awaiting the Arrival Family Time Training activity books. She loves any chance to empower parents as the primary spiritual trainers of their children through writing and training opportunities.

Jenna Hallock lives and serves with her husband, Mark, in Littleton, Colorado. She has been connected with the ministry of Family Time Training for over 15 years and loves to see what happens when parents start intentional home discipleship.

MATERIALS
LIST

EVERY WEEK:

- Advent candle
- Lighter or matches
- Memory verse card

SESSION ONE:

- A mug for each family member
- Hot chocolate mix
- Hot water in a teapot or kettle
- Marshmallows
- List of treasure hunt clues

SESSION TWO:

- Fort building materials: Chairs, blankets, Clothes pins (pegs)
- Dark colored sheet
- String of Christmas lights
- Pillows
- Flashlight (torch)
- Optional: Snack

SESSION THREE:

- Two evergreen scented items (i.e. candles, essential oil, potpourri, or, scented plug-in air freshener refill, car freshener trees, fresh evergreen sprigs)
- Five familiar scented items (i.e. orange peel, coffee grounds, peanut butter, fabric softener sheets, a favorite candle)
- Seven lunch-sized paper bags

SESSION FOUR:

- Optional: blanket for each person
- Small jar (baby food or small mason jars work great)
- Glitter
- Clear glue
- Warm water

SESSION FIVE:

- Blank cards
- Writing materials (crayons/markers/colored pencils)

SCRIPTURE MEMORY TIPS AND TRICKS

- Memorizing Scripture does not need to be overwhelming. Many families love memorizing Scripture together and we hope these tips and tricks will make this life skill more fun for your family!

- Write the Scripture verse on a small card and place it in your car. Every time your family goes somewhere, have someone read the verse aloud, but read it call-and-response style – read one phrase and have everyone else repeat the phrase and so on throughout the entire verse.

- Write the Scripture verse in dry erase marker on the bathroom mirrors and challenge family members to read through the verse three times while brushing their teeth.

- Write the Scripture verse on a whiteboard or chalkboard hanging in a central place in the home (kitchen or entryway). Challenge family members to read through the Scripture whenever they enter the room. Every few days erase one word from the passage and once in a while ask a family member to read the verse aloud including the missing words.

- Write the Scripture verse on small cards and hang them in a visible place in each family member's room – mirrors and bulletin boards work well.

- Write the Scripture verse on cardstock paper cut into bookmarks and place one in each family member's Bible.

- Google "Isaiah 9:6 song" and you'll find a few versions you could play for your family to help them memorize the verse.

- After a month of practicing the memory verse, play "Back-and-Forth" with your children. To play this game, you and your child will say every other word of the verse until you recite the entire verse together. For example,

Parent: "For"

Child: "To"

Parent: "Us"

Child: "A"

Parent: "Child"

1

COMMUNITY ENGAGEMENT IDEAS

 **PLAY TIME WITH LITTLE ONES**

Using stuffed animals or action figures, act out scenarios of telling others that Jesus loves them and inviting them to church. Children who practice sharing Jesus with toys are more likely to share Him with real people.

🎆 GO TIME

Start relationships with people who have children and teens your children's ages. Invite them to do family activities with your family. You can do things like going to the playground, having a board games night, or even going to the zoo together. The goal with building these relationships is to shine Jesus' light and invite those families to come and see Him at work in your family's life.

 MEAL TIME

Choose one family who has not, yet, committed to following Jesus to pray for before each family meal for a month. Then toward the end of the month invite that family to share a meal with you and see where the Holy Spirit leads your conversation.

 BED TIME

Pray with your children for at least one of their friends who has not, yet, accepted Jesus' gift of salvation before bed each night. Challenge them to serve and be kind to that child the next time they are together.

TRAINING AND EQUIPPING
FAMILIES

- BIBLICALLY-BASED
- ENCOURAGING & FUN
- PRACTICAL & IMPACTFUL

HOST A **FAMILY TIME TRAINING**
EVENT IN YOUR COMMUNITY

FAMILY TIME
TRAINING

famtime.com

More from 10Publishing

Resources that point to Jesus

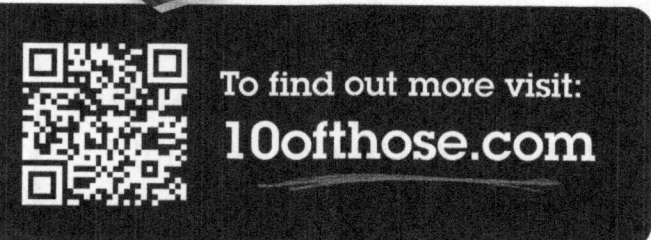